WITH HIM, I AM SAFE!

7 Day Devotional

NIKAYLA A. BENBOW

Copyright © 2025 by Nikayla A. Benbow

All rights reserved. This book or any portion thereof may not be reproduced or used in any manner whatsoever without the express written permission of the publisher except for the use of brief quotations in a book review.

Printed in the United States of America

First Edition, 2025

PAPERBACK ISBN: 979-8-3493-4638-5

EBOOK ISBN: 979-8-3493-4639-2

Red Pen Edits and Consulting

www.redpeneditsllc.com

CONTENTS

DEDICATIONS	*1*
INTRODUCTION	*5*
DAY ONE	
Breakups and Heartbreak	*7*
DAY TWO	
Doubt and Uncertainty	*15*
DAY THREE	
Financial Struggles	*27*
DAY FOUR	
Fear and Anxiety	*41*
DAY FIVE	
Healing from Trauma	*53*
DAY SIX	
Self-Esteem Issues	*67*

DAY SEVEN
    Anger and Frustration   *79*

REFERENCES   *89*

ABOUT THE AUTHOR   *91*

DEDICATIONS

First and foremost, I want to take this sacred moment to thank my true Lord and Savior, Jesus Christ, for the opportunity to share my heart and understanding with the world. Without Him, I would be nothing, and through Him, I can do all things! His love for me is boundless and unwavering, even when I fall short. He is my constant, my refuge, and my greatest inspiration. I could write endlessly about His love and faithfulness, but let's move on to honor the incredible souls He has placed in my life to help bring this journal/book to fruition.

To My Leaders, Apostle Gary and Myra Bellinger

Thank you from the depths of my heart for your teachings, your wisdom, and your unwavering devotion to the Word of God. Since joining City of God Ministries International in Concord, NC, my life has been transformed in ways I never imagined possible. Your examples of faith, integrity, and extraordinary leadership inspire me daily. Thank you for creating a space where truth reigns, love abounds, and God's presence is felt so strongly. I am forever grateful to be under your covering.

To My Amazing Parents, Richard and Angela Robinson

You are my anchors and my greatest cheerleaders. You have walked with me through every storm, celebrated my victories, and never stopped believing in me, even when I struggled to believe in myself. The laughter we've shared, the lessons you've taught, and the love you've poured into me have shaped me into the woman I am today. You've shown me the power of forgiveness, faith, and perseverance. Thank you for teaching me that no matter how far I stray, God's arms—and yours—are always open to me.

To My Precious Son, My Heart And My Greatest Gift

Thank you for giving me the beautiful title of Mom. Being your mother has been my most sacred calling and my deepest joy. You've taught me a love I never knew existed, one that challenges me to be better every day. Because of you, I dream bigger, love harder, and stand stronger. No matter where life takes you, no matter the highs or lows you face, always remember this: I will forever be your greatest supporter, your unwavering protector, and your constant source of love.

To The Safe Place MVMT Ladies, My Sisters In Christ

You are a treasure. You walked alongside me through the challenges of this journey, wiping my tears, lifting my spirits, and encouraging me to press forward when I felt like giving up. Your faith in me and your commitment to this God-given vision have been nothing short of miraculous. Together, we are breaking chains, healing hearts, and creating a sanctuary for those in need. Thank you for standing with me through every transition and for reminding me that with God, no vision is too big, and no mission is impossible.

To anyone who reads these words, know this:

You are loved, you are chosen, and you have a purpose. May the words in this book touch your heart, guide your steps, and remind you that God's grace is sufficient for you in every season of life.

INTRODUCTION

Have you ever trusted God, but when life gets tough, it seems like He is nowhere to be found? Or does it feel like everything that could go wrong is going wrong? Your job is stressing you out, the kids are acting crazy, your spouse seems to have a special knack for pushing your buttons, you feel unimportant, and someone you thought you could trust ends up hurting you? I know I've been there more times than I can count!

The intention of this 7-day devotional is to remind you that **YOU ARE NOT ALONE!** We have unlimited access to the Holy Spirit. Over the next seven days, we will explore real-life examples of just how involved the Holy Spirit can be in your life—if you let Him. You'll learn that the weight of the world doesn't have to rest on your shoulders, but is carried on His. In John 16:7, Jesus says:

"However, I am telling you nothing but the truth when I say it is profitable (good, expedient, advantageous) for you

that I go away. Because if I do not go away, the Comforter (Counselor, Helper, Advocate, Intercessor, Strengthener, Standby) will not come to you [into close fellowship with you]; but if I go, I will send Him to you [to be in close fellowship with you]."

Jesus knew that we couldn't live this life without the assistance, reassurance, and support of the Holy Spirit. God has called you to a place of wholeness and peace, but it can only be fully established through an intimate relationship with Him. God's purpose is never to hurt you, but to heal you.

Throughout this devotional, I'll share a bit of my own story and how I came to realize that I needed the Holy Spirit more than I ever thought.

Come, let's take this walk together…

Day One

BREAKUPS AND HEARTBREAK

Heartbreak leaves us feeling shattered and alone. I remember a specific time in my life when I experienced some of the worst breakups and heartache. I remember sitting on the floor, asking God why He would allow such pain. I became angry with God, and honestly, I doubted His abilities.

One thing God showed me in that season was that I had never given the Holy Spirit the opportunity to be the Comforter He truly is. I was desperately seeking comfort from others, which only led to disappointment and more heartbreak. The pain from those events allowed me to finally see how much the Holy Spirit cares for and loves me.

During this time of transition, I had to unlearn behaviors that I had subjected myself to and learn what true love and support look like through the Holy Spirit. I had to realize that during these hard moments, the Holy Spirit wanted to be my Comforter. He wanted to be with me—little old me. He cared about my heart, my mental state, and my well-being. He wasn't too "High and Mighty" to help me.

For the first time in my life, I no longer saw Him through the lens of rigid religious teachings. He wasn't a mystical being, distant and hard to approach. I finally saw Him as a friend, someone who actually cared about me.

> *"The Lord is close to the brokenhearted and saves those who are crushed in spirit."*
>
> **Psalm 34:18**

Heartbreak leaves us feeling shattered and alone. But during those times, the Holy Spirit wants to be your comforter. Invite Him into your pain. Sit in silence, and let Him speak to your spirit, reminding you that even in this loss, you are never truly alone.

The Relational Nature of the Holy Spirit

> *"The Spirit of the Lord is upon me… He has sent me to bind up the brokenhearted."*
> **Isaiah 61:1**

The Holy Spirit's nature is to heal. He is deeply invested in your restoration and wholeness. Though the pain of a breakup feels overwhelming, He is gently mending your heart, piece by piece. He doesn't rush the process, but when it's complete, He will bring healing that transforms your heartache into hope. Though your heart feels broken, the Holy Spirit is at work, restoring it with divine care. He's not just patching the wounds—He's making you whole in ways you never imagined. Trust Him to bring beauty from the ashes.

Cultivating Intimacy with the Holy Spirit

Instead of running from the pain, invite the Holy Spirit into it. He wants to sit with you in your heartache and listen to you, offering His presence as medicine for your soul. When you cry out to Him, He draws near, filling the emptiness with

His love. Your pain is not too much for God. The Holy Spirit desires to meet you right where you are. Bring your tears, your confusion, and your hurt to Him, and experience His healing presence.

Understanding His Personality and Role

The Holy Spirit wraps His presence around your wounded heart, bringing peace that surpasses understanding. Unlike human comfort, His presence gives you steady, unshakable strength that cannot be broken no matter how hard life gets. When the world leaves you feeling empty, the Holy Spirit fills that emptiness with a love that cannot be lost or erased. In your tears, He is there, reminding you that you are seen, cherished, and never alone.

Final Thoughts on Engaging with the Holy Spirit

In the middle of your heartbreak, the Holy Spirit whispers hope, provides strength, and reassures you. Ask Him to fill the empty places in your heart with His presence, giving you peace and understanding beyond the pain.

REFLECTION QUESTIONS

How can you finally let go and allow the Holy Spirit full access to your heart?

_____

_____

_____

_____

_____

In what areas do you need the Holy Spirit's help the most?

_____

_____

_____

_____

_____

PRACTICAL APPLICATION

Healing from heartbreak and breakups is a painful but transformative journey. Building a relationship with the Holy Spirit during this time can offer deep comfort, strength, and wisdom. Here is a practical application to help overcome heartbreak, along with a motivational reflection to guide you.

Allow the Holy Spirit to Heal Your Heart

Ask the Holy Spirit to bring healing to the wounds left by the breakup. Be honest with Him about your pain, and trust that He will begin the process of restoration in your heart. Take steps to care for your emotional health, knowing that healing is a journey. Healing doesn't happen overnight, but the Holy Spirit is actively working within you. Trust in His power to restore and renew your heart, making you stronger than before.

PRAYER

Heavenly Father,

I come before You with a heavy heart, carrying the pain and sorrow of this breakup. Lord, You know the depth of my hurt, and I lay it all before You, trusting that You understand my pain more than anyone else. I ask for Your healing touch to mend my broken heart and to restore my spirit.

Holy Spirit, I invite You to guide me through this difficult time. Help me to surrender my emotions to You and trust in Your perfect plan. Please remind me of my worth in You and teach me to lean on Your presence for comfort and strength. In moments of loneliness and sadness, may I find peace in knowing that You are always with me, and that Your love is unwavering.

Lord, I desire to grow closer to You through this pain. Teach me how to turn to You instead of relying on earthly things for comfort. May this heartbreak draw me into a deeper relationship with You, as I learn to find my identity and security in

Your love alone. Fill me with Your peace and joy that surpasses all understanding.

I trust that You will heal my heart in Your perfect time and help me to move forward with hope, knowing that You have something greater planned for me. Thank You for Your unfailing love and for the strength You provide through Your Holy Spirit.

In Jesus' name, I pray,

Amen.

Day Two

DOUBT AND UNCERTAINTY

Oftentimes, we find ourselves in a place called doubt and uncertainty. This place can be very dark and hopeless, feeling like a bottomless pit from which there's no escape. As I sit here writing this entry, I realize that I've frequently struggled with these emotions throughout my adult years. One of the leading causes of these feelings is when I'm forced to make a decision—whether to consider a job offer, question my capabilities as a parent, or doubt my ability to be a good person. I often find myself doubting who I am as a Child of God, beating the enemy to the punch by counting myself out before he even has a chance.

This vicious cycle can be incredibly damaging—not only to our natural hearts and minds but also to our spirits! How can we say, "God, I trust You and believe what You have said about me," but then, in the same breath, turn around and say, "I don't think I can do this"? See, doubt and belief cannot exist in the same space. When doubt and uncertainty start to arise in your life, you must ask yourself a very important question: "What is my true belief system?"

When I refer to a belief system, I'm talking about your spirit's position on the matter in which you feel doubt or uncertainty. While walking with the Holy Spirit through this particular season in my life, He brought to my attention that in order to reach a place of peace, I needed to have the right belief system. What does that look like, you ask? It looks like trust, dependency, and unwavering love in God, no matter what.

The scripture I'm providing you with was one of the main scriptures I had plastered in my brain and on my bathroom mirror! I had to learn that the only way I could finally win this war was to **TRULY trust in the Lord with ALL of my heart** and not lean on my own understanding! I had to physically raise my hands and outwardly say, "God,

I trust You with this." Tears would often fall from my eyes because my natural abilities couldn't comprehend this act of faith, but my spirit would leap with excitement because I was actively offering up my troubles to my Father.

It was difficult at times to keep this up, and I would beat myself up for even being in that space. However, the Holy Spirit kept reassuring me that as I offered my burdens to Him, He was working it all out. I learned that I didn't have to continue fighting this battle because **He fights for me!** So, I encourage you to finally put the gloves down and allow the Holy Spirit to fight for you! You no longer have to doubt because **He is SURE!**

> *"Trust in the Lord with all your heart and lean not on your own understanding; in all your ways submit to Him, and He will make your paths straight."*
>
> **Proverbs 3:5-6**

Doubt creeps in when life feels uncertain. The Holy Spirit gently reminds you that God's plans are higher than yours. His ways are not your ways. His thoughts are not your thoughts. Even when you can't see the full picture, He is working things out for your good.

The Relational Nature of the Holy Spirit

> *"But when the Spirit of truth comes, He will guide you into all truth."*
>
> **John 16:13**

Changes can cause self-doubt, leading you to question your capabilities. The Holy Spirit, as the Spirit of Truth, reassures you of who you are in Christ. He speaks truth into your circumstances, reminding you that you are loved, chosen, and valued by God, regardless of how bad the situation may be. The Holy Spirit clears the fog of doubt and confusion, reminding you of the unchanging truth—that you are deeply loved by God and that your victory is secure in His hands, no matter how hard the experience may get.

Cultivating Intimacy with the Holy Spirit

> *"But you will receive power when the Holy Spirit comes on you."*
> **Acts 1:8**

Hardships and challenges sometimes leave us feeling weak and drained. Cultivate intimacy with the Holy Spirit by acknowledging your weakness and relying on His strength. He will empower you to take the next step, face each day, and begin the healing process of finally letting go. Leaning on Him allows His power to be made perfect in your weakness. The Holy Spirit doesn't ask you to be strong on your own. He is your strength. In your weakness, He will empower you, giving you what you need to endure and eventually rise above the battle.

Understanding His Personality and Role

> *"May the God of hope fill you with all joy and peace as you trust in Him, so that you may overflow with hope by the power of the Holy Spirit."*
>
> **Romans 15:13**

In the midst of challenges, it's easy to lose hope. Yet the Holy Spirit is the wellspring of hope that never runs dry. He fills you with fresh hope for the future, reminding you that God is always working for your good, even in the battle. He helps you see that this season will not define your life, but it will lead to a new and beautiful chapter. Your hope is not in a person or in yourself, but in the unshakable promises of God. The Holy Spirit fills you with hope, knowing that God has plans to prosper you, to give you hope and a future. He is the only true and living source of Hope.

Final Thoughts on Engaging with the Holy Spirit

Doubt creeps in when life feels uncertain. The Holy Spirit gently reminds you that God's plans are higher than yours. Even when you can't see the full picture, He is working things out for your good. So, take your hands off, remove the restraints on your faith, and watch Him work! Ask the Holy Spirit to guide you step by step through uncertainty. His presence is the assurance that you are never navigating this life alone.

REFLECTION QUESTIONS

In what areas of your life are you experiencing doubt and uncertainty?

_____

_____

_____

_____

_____

Do you believe that God has you?

_____

_____

_____

_____

_____

What is your belief system?

_____

_____

_____

_____

_____

What would you change about it to mirror the power of God moving in that area?

_____

_____

_____

_____

_____

PRACTICAL APPLICATION

Overcoming doubt and uncertainty can be one of life's greatest challenges, but building a relationship with the Holy Spirit brings peace, guidance, and clarity. Here is a practical application, paired with a motivational reflection to help you navigate through uncertainty with confidence:

Invite the Holy Spirit into Your Doubts

When you experience doubt, rather than turning inward or trying to handle it alone, invite the Holy Spirit to guide you through the uncertainty. Take a moment to pray, "Holy Spirit, I am uncertain, but I trust You to lead me. Please bring clarity and peace." The Holy Spirit is not afraid of your doubts. He is here to guide you with wisdom and understanding, helping you to see beyond your limitations and trust in God's faithfulness.

PRAYER

Heavenly Father,

I come before You in my moments of uncertainty and doubt, seeking Your guidance and peace. Lord, You know the struggles I face, and I confess that I often feel lost and unsure of the path ahead. But I trust that You are with me, and You hold my future in Your hands. I surrender my fears and doubts to You, knowing that You are faithful to lead me.

Holy Spirit, I invite You into my heart and mind. I ask You to fill me with Your wisdom and discernment, to help me trust in God's plans for my life. In times when uncertainty clouds my vision, remind me that You are my guide and that You will never leave me. Teach me to rely on Your presence and to listen closely to Your voice.

Lord, I desire to deepen my relationship with You. Help me to walk by faith and not by sight, trusting that You are working behind the scenes even when I cannot see it. Strengthen my trust in Your timing and Your purpose for my life. Help me to find peace in knowing that You are always with me, guiding me, and loving me.

I thank You for Your constant presence and for the Holy Spirit, who leads me in all truth. May my heart grow closer to You, and may my faith in You become unshakable, even in the face of uncertainty.

In Jesus' name, I pray,

Amen.

Day Three

FINANCIAL STRUGGLES

When finances are tight or nonexistent, emotions such as worry, fear, and sadness can easily take hold. It's easy to feel like God isn't providing or doesn't hear you. Yet the Holy Spirit can remind you that your true security isn't in money but in God's ability to provide. Whew, there's nothing more challenging than when your money is looking funny!

I've found that alongside love, this is one of the prominent areas where the enemy attacks me. Throughout my adult years, I've experienced countless drought-like seasons. Bill collectors would call nonstop, and I'd go to the store with anxiety, unsure if my card would go through. So many times, I panicked and tried to "figure it out," but looking back, I realize, I was just digging a bigger hole for myself.

Why was it so hard to trust God with this area of my life? Why did it feel like I could never catch a break when it came to not having enough? Why was living paycheck to paycheck my norm? These are just a few of the many questions I asked God while crying in the middle of my closet floor. I couldn't understand how I was blessed when everything around me seemed to show the total opposite. I thought my life wasn't reflecting overflow and abundance, but oh, how wrong I was!

The Holy Spirit "chin-checked" me and asked, "Have you gone homeless? Have you been without food? Have your lights been cut off? Has your child starved?" And a series of other gut-wrenching realities that I had failed to appreciate at the time. What He taught me was that I had found my identity in a job and not fully in God. Because of this, I subconsciously believed my source was the employer, not my Heavenly Father.

For so long, I kept God in a box, believing He could work wonders in every area of my life EXCEPT my finances and love life. I had somehow convinced myself that God was too big to worry about small things like my job and the resources I needed. This thought process was eating me up inside and preventing me from seeing the truth in the scripture below!

See, I thought my needs were limited to the natural list I presented to God, but it's much deeper than that! God only requires us to live IN Him as much as we can. I didn't have to "figure it out"—that's His job! I didn't have to make ends meet—that's His job! I didn't need to have sleepless nights! His riches in glory through Christ Jesus are all I need. Those riches include established peace, love, and abundance. Everything I needed was rooted in Him having full control over every area of my life, and in that comes wealth, health, and wholeness! He never asked me to do anything except to be IN Him.

So I encourage you today, let His riches shine in that rough place in your life. When I finally decided to let go and allow God full access, my language and habits changed from worry and fear to appreciation and praise! I no longer saw a bill due; instead, I saw an opportunity for God to show Himself in my life. And at the right time, IT WILL BE TAKEN CARE OF. And guess what? Even if it's not, **HE IS STILL GOOD!**

He cares for you, He does not wish bad or harm on you, He sees it ALL, and He hears your cries. I promise, if you turn it over to Him, He will NOT let you down!

> *"And my God will meet all your needs according to the riches of His glory in Christ Jesus."*
> **Philippians 4:19**

When finances are tight, worry can feel overwhelming. It's easy to feel like God isn't providing or isn't hearing you. Yet the Holy Spirit can remind you that your true security isn't in money but in God's ability to provide.

The Relational Nature of the Holy Spirit

> *"Cast all your anxiety on Him because He cares for you."*
> **1 Peter 5:7**

In the midst of financial struggles, when it feels like everything is falling apart, the Holy Spirit sustains you. He carries your burdens, holds you together, and gives you the grace to face each day. You don't have to carry the weight of worry alone—He is your strength and support. When life feels overwhelming and things seem not to be working in your favor, the Holy Spirit is holding you up, sustaining you through each moment. His care for you is constant and unwavering, giving you the strength to keep moving forward, even when things feel too heavy.

Cultivating Intimacy with the Holy Spirit

> *"But those who wait on the Lord shall renew their strength; they shall mount up with wings like eagles, they shall run and not be weary, they shall walk and not faint."*
>
> **Isaiah 40:31**

Believing God is a process, and intimacy with the Holy Spirit takes time. Be patient and trust that as you wait on Him, He is renewing your strength and preparing your heart for new beginnings. Let the waiting be a time of reestablishing your connection with Him. God is not in a rush, and neither is the Holy Spirit. Wait on Him, trusting that He is renewing you, and in His perfect timing, you will soar again with new strength and hope.

Understanding His Personality and Role

> *"You have turned my mourning into dancing; You have removed my sackcloth and clothed me with joy."*
>
> **Psalm 30:11**

The Holy Spirit not only relieves your anxiety but also restores your joy. In time, He will take the worry you feel today and replace it with joy unspeakable. While the process may seem slow, His work is deep and transformational, ensuring that joy WILL return to your life in ways you couldn't imagine. Yes, Joy is coming! Even if it seems distant now, the Holy Spirit promises to restore your laughter and dancing. He is turning your mourning into a testimony of God's faithfulness and grace.

Final Thoughts on Engaging with the Holy Spirit

In times of financial struggle, invite the Holy Spirit to guide you in wisdom—trusting Him and letting go—to open doors that no one can close and to give you peace as you wait for God's provision to show up in your life. This process is not easy, but

I can testify that when done with God, He will complete it!

REFLECTION QUESTIONS

Are you currently in a season of waiting on God to answer your financial concerns?

_____

_____

_____

_____

_____

Why is it so hard for you to trust God with your finances?

_____

_____

_____

_____

_____

What financial habits do you have that need God's assistance?

_____

_____

_____

_____

_____

Are you truly ready to be and do better with your finances?

_____

_____

_____

_____

_____

PRACTICAL APPLICATION

> *"I can do all this through Him who gives me strength."*
> **Philippians 4:13**

In moments when you feel overwhelmed, remember to lean on the Holy Spirit for strength. Whether it's getting through the day or facing a difficult situation, trust that He will give you the inner strength to gain victory over it. Your strength comes from the Holy Spirit, not from yourself. Trust that He will uphold you and give you the power to overcome even the toughest seasons.

PRAYER

Heavenly Father,

I come before You with a heart full of frustration and worry over my financial struggles. Lord, You know the weight that this burden places on my mind and spirit, and I trust You to hear my cry. I lay my concerns at Your feet, knowing that You are my provider and that You care for every need in my life.

Holy Spirit, I invite You to guide me in this season. Help me to release my anxieties and fears, and to trust in Your provision. Teach me to manage the resources I have with wisdom and faithfulness, and show me the steps I can take to improve my situation. Remind me that, even in moments of financial difficulty, You are present with me, providing the strength and peace I need.

Lord, I desire to grow deeper in my relationship with You. May this financial challenge draw me closer to You, as I learn to rely on You more fully. Teach me to trust in Your timing, to be patient, and to remember that my true security is found in You alone, not in my circumstances.

Fill me with the peace that surpasses understanding, and help me to shift my focus from worry to gratitude. Help me to trust that You are always at work, even when I don't see the immediate answers. Strengthen my faith, and let my heart be open to the guidance of Your Spirit in all areas of my life.

Thank You, Lord, for Your unwavering love and faithfulness. I trust that You will provide for me, not just in this moment, but always. I surrender my worries to You, knowing that You are working all things for my good.

In Jesus' name, I pray,

Amen!

Day Four

FEAR AND ANXIETY

What is fear? What is anxiety? According to dictionary.com, *fear* is defined as "to be afraid of (someone or something) as likely to be dangerous, painful, or threatening." *Anxiety* is intense, excessive, and persistent worry and fear about everyday situations. Symptoms may include a fast heart rate, rapid breathing, sweating, and feeling tired.

How many times have you found yourself experiencing these emotions over something or someone? When I think back to past days, and even now sometimes, I find myself back in those spaces—crippled by fear and anxiety, feeling like there was no way out. Anything could trigger these emotions: my child, friends, family, decisions, or even a past obstacle resurfacing. It all felt like the pain was happening all over again.

For years, fear and anxiety were my default coping mechanisms. They became my "comfort zones." By that, I mean it was so easy to fall into them whenever a challenge arose in my life. They became my first responders, my spokespersons, my way of life. I didn't know any better. I would just wait for the storm to pass, hoping I'd go back to normal until the next wave hit, repeating the cycle.

Being trapped in these emotions for years kept me stuck. I didn't even realize I was in this vicious cycle until I developed an intimate relationship with the Holy Spirit. Yes, the cycle of allowing these emotions to control me came to a halt for the first time in my life! Now, I'm not saying they completely vanished, but with the help of the Holy Spirit, I no longer felt crippled or silenced when they showed up. I learned to fight back and take authority over them.

How do you do that, you may ask? I simply prayed:

"Holy Spirit, I know this is not a battle I have to fight anymore because You are with me. You have all power and understanding. You told me in Your Word, God, that You

will never leave me nor forsake me, and right now, these emotions are trying to disrupt the truth with lies. So come into this decision-making process, this relationship, this motherhood—take full control. I understand that I cannot fight this with my own strength, but it is Your strength that causes me to win this battle. Here, have it!"

As I say this exact prayer, I raise my hands in surrender, palms up, and exhale. What I've noticed is that as soon as I physically, mentally, and emotionally let go, I feel an overwhelming sense of peace instantly! I would never have known this peace was possible if I hadn't learned the importance of having oneness with the Holy Spirit!

Of course, fear and anxiety still rear their heads, but no matter how many times they come, I vow to say this prayer, even today! You don't have to be a slave to these emotions if you don't want to—there is another way! God wants us to have LIFE, and have it MORE ABUNDANTLY! We can't experience the abundance of life if fear and anxiety have control over us. You have NEW life through a deeper relationship with the Holy Spirit!

> *"For God has not given us a spirit of fear, but of power, and of love, and of a sound mind."*
> **2 Timothy 1:7**

Fear can cripple us, but it's not from God. The Holy Spirit brings courage, peace, and understanding where fear seeks to overwhelm, confuse, and silence you. The Holy Spirit replaces anxiety with His gentle presence, calming your soul.

The Relational Nature of the Holy Spirit

> *"Cast all your anxiety on Him because He cares for you."*
> **1 Peter 5:7**

In the midst of fear and anxiety, when it feels like everything is falling apart, the Holy Spirit keeps you. He carries your burdens, holds you together, and gives you the grace to face each day. You don't have to carry the weight of your situation alone because He is your strength and support. When life feels overwhelming, the Holy Spirit is holding you up, sustaining you through each moment. His care for you is constant and unwavering, giving you the strength to keep moving forward, even when the weight of fear and anxiety feels too heavy.

Cultivating Intimacy with the Holy Spirit

> *"Be still, and know that I am God."*
> **Psalm 46:10**

In uncertain times, your mind may race with anxious thoughts and "what-ifs." Cultivate intimacy with the Holy Spirit by spending time in stillness. In the quiet, you make room to hear His voice, which whispers peace, comfort, and assurance into your soul. Silence may feel uncomfortable, but it is in the stillness that the Holy Spirit speaks most clearly. Let His presence fill the quiet spaces, and in that quiet, find rest and renewal for your soul.

Understanding His Personality and Role

> *"Peace I leave with you; My peace I give you. I do not give to you as the world gives. Do not let your hearts be troubled, and do not be afraid."*
>
> **John 14:27**

In the chaos and turmoil of not knowing what's next, the Holy Spirit brings supernatural peace. This peace isn't based on circumstances, but is rooted in the unchanging presence of God. When your emotions swirl out of control, He steadies your heart and quiets your fears and anxieties.

Final Thoughts on Engaging with the Holy Spirit

Peace is a gift from the Holy Spirit. When you're challenged by fear and anxiety, it's sometimes hard to believe there is an opportunity for peace. Even when circumstances are difficult, trust that His peace will surpass your understanding, and it will establish you in God's unwavering love.

REFLECTION QUESTIONS

How can you release the fear and anxiety over the situations in your life?

_____

_____

_____

_____

_____

How can you show God that you surrender to Him today?

_____

_____

_____

_____

_____

What areas in your life do you trust God to take full control over?

_____

_____

_____

_____

_____

PRACTICAL APPLICATION:

> *"And the peace of God, which transcends all understanding, will guard your hearts and your minds in Christ Jesus."*
>
> **Philippians 4:7**

True peace comes from trusting the Holy Spirit with your heart and your future. When anxiety and fear creep in, take a moment to breathe deeply and ask the Holy Spirit to fill you with His peace. Trust that He will guard your heart and mind, bringing calmness to your soul.

PRAYER

Heavenly Father,

I come before You with a heart full of fear and anxiety. Lord, You know the worries that consume me and the overwhelming thoughts that take hold of my mind. In this moment, I choose to lay my fears at Your feet, knowing that You are the one who holds my life in Your hands. I ask for Your peace to fill my heart, and Your presence to calm the storm within me.

Holy Spirit, I invite You to dwell within me more deeply. Help me to remember that You are my comforter and my guide. When fear threatens to take over, remind me that I do not walk alone. Teach me to trust in Your perfect love, for Your Word says that perfect love casts out fear. Help me to draw nearer to You, to be sensitive to Your presence, and to listen to Your still, small voice that speaks peace to my soul.

Lord, I desire to know You more and to experience the fullness of Your Spirit. In my moments of anxiety, teach me to turn to You, not to the distractions or worries of this world. Help me to rely on Your strength when I am weak, to rest in Your promises, and to find my security in Your unwavering love.

Fill me with the peace that only You can give, and help me to walk in faith rather than fear. May my relationship with You grow deeper, and may Your Spirit lead me into a life of freedom, trusting You in every circumstance.

Thank You, Lord, for Your constant presence and Your faithfulness. I surrender my fear and anxiety to You, knowing that You are in control and that Your perfect peace will guard my heart and mind.

In Jesus' name, I pray,

Amen!

Day Five

HEALING FROM TRAUMA

Out of all the devotional days listed above, this particular subject is one that I am currently working on with the Holy Spirit, so you get to walk with me as I, too, walk with the Holy Spirit. Healing. What is healing? How do you know when you are being led to it? How do you welcome it into your life? These are all questions that I have and am still currently asking the Holy Spirit, and He has been answering them daily!

For imagery purposes, healing seemed to me like a door that was wide open but far across the room. No matter how many steps I took toward it, I could never reach it. I felt as if healing was not something I could ever fully grasp and walk in because the trauma would inconveniently block me. This was a battle that I found myself fighting for years and even recently! I thank God for the Holy Spirit!

Because NOW, I am learning that healing is not some impossible "task" that I will never complete; it is obtainable and well-deserved, no matter what I did! I am not exempt or disqualified from being totally healed from trauma. The guilt and condemnation of my past and even my current mistakes do not define my sonship with God. He loves me. I am reminded of the scripture Psalm 34:18-19 AMP: "The Lord is near to the heartbroken and saves those who are crushed in spirit (contrite in heart, truly sorry for their sin). Many hardships and perplexing circumstances confront the righteous, but the Lord rescues him from them all." He is concerned about the traumas I have experienced, and He wants to rescue me from the grip of shame and embarrassment that these things bring. I am healing from trauma, and I now encourage you to insert yourself in this entry and allow God the same access so He, too, can offer you total healing!

> *"He heals the brokenhearted and binds up their wounds."*
>
> **Psalm 147:3**

Trauma leaves deep wounds, but the Holy Spirit is a healer. He patiently walks with you through the process, bringing restoration to the broken places. Though healing takes time, His presence ensures you don't walk that path alone.

The Relational Nature of the Holy Spirit

Healing from trauma requires more than just human effort; it is a process of surrender, of letting go, and allowing the Holy Spirit to work within us, gently mending brokenness, restoring hope, and strengthening our spirit. The Holy Spirit brings not only comfort but also wisdom and remembrance of God's promises. In the midst of trauma, we may forget who we are, feel lost, or carry wounds that seem too heavy. But the Holy Spirit reminds us of our identity in Christ—beloved, whole, and redeemed.

Through the Spirit, we find the courage to confront pain, trusting that we are not alone in it. The Spirit walks with us, even in our darkest moments, breathing new life into us, renewing our minds, and reawakening joy and peace. The Holy Spirit's relational nature means we are always accompanied, always understood, and always loved. With every step we take toward healing, the Spirit is there, guiding us into greater freedom and wholeness. Let your spirit be open to this transformative companionship, for with the Holy Spirit, there is always hope and healing.

Cultivating Intimacy with the Holy Spirit

During a season of healing from trauma, cultivating intimacy with the Holy Spirit is a sacred journey, one that requires an open heart and a willingness to invite God's presence into even the most wounded places. Healing from trauma is often painful, but with the Holy Spirit as our companion, it can also become an experience of great transformation. The Spirit desires to draw near, to comfort, and to guide us into deeper wholeness.

One way to cultivate this intimacy is through quiet moments of prayer and stillness, allowing yourself to listen and rest in God's presence. Even when words fail, the Holy Spirit prays on our behalf, understanding every unspoken need, every silent tear, and every hidden wound. In stillness, we can feel the Spirit's gentle comfort and the assurance that we are understood and held. Healing is not a journey you take alone; it is one that the Holy Spirit walks with you, guiding you toward deeper intimacy, peace, and restoration. Even in the midst of pain, the Holy Spirit is there, offering a presence that heals, restores, and transforms.

Understanding His Personality and Role

In the same way, the Spirit helps us in our weakness. We do not know what we ought to pray for, but the Spirit Himself intercedes for us through wordless groans. — *Romans 8:26*

Sometimes, trauma can leave you speechless, unable to even express your pain to God. The Holy Spirit is your Advocate, interceding on your behalf when words fail. He knows the depth of your traumatic experiences and prays for you with groanings too deep for words, willingly carrying your burden to the Father. Even when you don't know what to say, the Holy Spirit is speaking on your behalf. He knows your heart and pleads your case before God. You are never alone in your pain, for the Spirit is always advocating for your healing and restoration.

Final Thoughts on Engaging with the Holy Spirit

Worship is a powerful way to engage with the Spirit. Even in your pain, when you lift your voice or even sit in silence, you invite the Holy Spirit to move within you. Worship shifts our focus, lifting us beyond our immediate pain and into God's presence. It can bring life changing comfort and clarity, helping us see beyond the trauma and look towards hope. You must trust that the Spirit will guide you in wisdom and patience. Healing doesn't happen all at once; it unfolds gradually as we stay close to God. Ask the Holy Spirit to reveal truths you need to hear, to guide your steps, and to strengthen you daily. As you open yourself to this divine guidance, you'll find comfort, strength, and renewed joy.

REFLECTION QUESTIONS

What burdens am I carrying that I can surrender to the Holy Spirit today?

_____

_____

_____

_____

_____

Where in my heart do I feel the most broken, and how can I invite the Holy Spirit into this space?

_____

_____

_____

_____

_____

How has God been present for me, even in moments of deep pain?

_____

_____

_____

_____

_____

What lies or negative beliefs have I held onto because of my trauma, and how can I replace them with God's truth?

_____

_____

_____

_____

_____

How can I show myself compassion and grace, as God does, while I heal?

_____

_____

_____

_____

_____

PRACTICAL APPLICATION

Here is one practical way to build a relationship with the Holy Spirit while healing from trauma. This practice is founded in scripture and created to be inspirational and empowering as you allow the Holy Spirit to bring comfort, renewal, and strength to your journey.

Create a "Healing Scriptures" Journal

Write down scriptures that speak to your heart about God's healing, love, and strength. When you're feeling discouraged, open your journal and meditate on these verses. Let the Holy Spirit illuminate the words and bring them to life, encouraging and comforting you. Regularly returning to God's promises helps anchor you in truth, even when emotions feel overwhelming.

PRAYER

Heavenly Father,

I come before You, humbly seeking Your strength and guidance. You know my heart, my struggles, and the doubts that weigh on me. Lord, I feel uncertain of my own worth, and my self-esteem is often shaken. Help me to see myself through Your eyes – as Your beloved child, created with purpose and value.

Holy Spirit, I invite You into my heart and mind to transform the way I see myself. Help me to replace fear with faith, insecurity with confidence, and self-doubt with trust in You. Remind me that my worth is not based on my achievements or others' opinions but on Your everlasting love.

Guide me, Holy Spirit, in building a deeper, more intimate relationship with You. Open my heart to Your truth, and fill my soul with Your peace. Teach me to lean on You for strength, wisdom, and confidence. When I feel weak, remind me that

You are my source of power. When I feel inadequate, remind me that I am made whole in You.

I ask for courage, Lord, to let go of negative thoughts about myself. Help me to speak words of life over my own heart, to build myself up as You would, with kindness and love. Let me see the gifts You have placed in me, and give me the strength to walk in them.

Thank You for loving me unconditionally and for never leaving my side. Help me to root my identity in You alone, and to find joy and confidence in Your presence. May my life be a reflection of Your grace, and may I grow closer to You each day.

In Jesus' name, I pray.

Amen!

Day Six

SELF-ESTEEM ISSUES

I think, as a woman, I can say that at some point throughout life, we all have or are actively struggling with self-esteem issues. Whether it was a person who chose someone else over you, a significant physical attribute that doesn't seem "attractive" to someone, or being turned down for a position because you did not look the part, there are so many silent but detrimental factors that contribute to this inward battle called self-esteem issues.

When walking with God and devoting myself to building an intimate relationship with the Holy Spirit, I discovered a few things about this particular struggle that I was unaware of. One of the things the Holy Spirit revealed to me was that my physical self-esteem issues translated to the spiritual realm, and in some way, I treated God as

I physically saw myself— inadequate. These issues hindered me from being able to see God as capable of using me or even blessing me because I felt I was not good enough or "anointed" enough to be used by God in a mighty way. The more I saw the incomplete parts of myself, the more I distanced myself from God and from truly seeking His face to understand how He sees me.

What the Holy Spirit gently reminded me of is that God is not like man or even like me. He sees me as beautiful, a masterpiece that He took His time on. He knew me before I was in my mother's womb. There is no way He could ever make a mistake or have an incomplete assignment—me. The Holy Spirit began to work on my viewpoint of God first and then myself.

I encourage you to really sit with today's entry and do the necessary work with the Holy Spirit to ensure that you, too, can begin to see yourself as God sees you!

> *"I praise You because I am fearfully and wonderfully made; Your works are wonderful, I know that full well."*
> **Psalm 139:14**

Low self-esteem distorts the truth about who we are in Christ. The Holy Spirit speaks to your spirit, confirming your identity as God's child. His presence affirms your worth, not based on what others say, but on who God says you are.

The Relational Nature of the Holy Spirit

When low self-esteem whispers that we're not enough, the Holy Spirit counters with a deep, divine assurance that we are "fearfully and wonderfully made" (Psalm 139:14). The Spirit guides us, helping us break free from the lies that hold us back, and instead, embrace the truth that we are loved unconditionally. Through the Spirit's gentle encouragement, we gain strength to stand tall, rooted in God's affirmation, empowered to love ourselves as He loves us. In this journey, we can rely on the Spirit to be our constant source of reassurance and peace, allowing us to live confidently, knowing we are valued, cherished, and never alone.

Cultivating Intimacy with the Holy Spirit

Cultivating intimacy with the Holy Spirit while struggling with self-esteem issues can be profoundly transformative. It begins with understanding that your worth is not defined by how you see yourself or how others perceive you but by how God sees you. The Holy Spirit is there to remind you of your divine value and purpose, and when you lean into that truth, it can lift the weight of self-doubt and insecurity. As you continue this journey, ask the Holy Spirit to guide you into seeing yourself as God sees you. He will empower you to overcome negative self-perceptions and reveal the beauty and strength within you. In His presence, you can find the confidence to stand tall, not in pride, but in the assurance that you are a beloved child of God, made for a purpose. Let this truth be the foundation on which you rebuild your self-esteem, with the Holy Spirit as your ever-present guide and friend.

Understanding His Personality and Role

The Holy Spirit's personality is gentle, compassionate, and deeply invested in guiding and comforting us, especially in our times of struggle and doubt. When facing self-esteem issues, the Spirit is like a wise friend who doesn't condemn but continually speaks words of encouragement, reminding us of our worth in God's eyes. The Holy Spirit doesn't criticize our weaknesses but instead empowers us, showing us that our identity isn't rooted in external validation or worldly standards but in the love and purpose God has placed within us. So whenever self-esteem struggles arise, remember this promise: "The Spirit you received does not make you slaves, so that you live in fear again; rather, the Spirit you received brought about your adoption to sonship. And by him, we cry, 'Abba, Father'" (Romans 8:15). In this, the Holy Spirit reassures us that we are not rejected or unworthy but are cherished children of God. We can find rest, value, and strength in that identity.

Final Thoughts on Engaging with the Holy Spirit

Isaiah 43:1 says, "Fear not, for I have redeemed you; I have called you by name, you are mine." When you struggle with self-esteem, remember that God knows you personally and claims you as His own. You're not just one among many; He has called you by name. This isn't about your outward achievements or status—it's about who you are in the eyes of your Creator. Ask the Holy Spirit to help you see yourself as God sees you. As you lean into His presence, you'll find the strength to reject self-doubt and embrace your identity as God's beloved. Keep returning to Scripture, asking the Spirit to illuminate its truths, and let Him guide you in building your confidence, not in yourself alone, but in the God who holds you close and calls you worthy.

REFLECTION QUESTIONS

How does God see me, and what qualities does He say I possess?

_____

_____

_____

_____

_____

Am I valuing myself according to the world's standards or God's standards?

_____

_____

_____

_____

_____

In what ways does my self-worth align with my identity as a child of God?

_____

_____

_____

_____

_____

How can I invite the Holy Spirit to guide my thoughts when I struggle with self-esteem?

_____

_____

_____

_____

_____

What purpose has God given me that can build my confidence?

_____

_____

_____

_____

_____

PRACTICAL APPLICATION

This is a practical way to build self-esteem through a closer relationship with the Holy Spirit. This application is designed to help you lean into God's love and see yourself as He sees you.

Daily Affirmations Inspired by Scripture

Spend a few minutes each morning affirming who you are in Christ. This practice helps renew your mind and builds your self-esteem by aligning your thoughts with God's truth. Write down a list of affirmations that reflect your identity in God. Examples include, "I am fearfully and wonderfully made" (Psalm 139:14) and "I am a child of God" (Romans 8:16). Meditate on these each morning, and ask the Holy Spirit to help you believe these truths deeply.

PRAYER

Heavenly Father,

I come before You with a heart that struggles with self-esteem and feelings of inadequacy. Lord, I confess that I often look at myself through the lens of my mistakes, shortcomings, and doubts, forgetting the truth of who You say I am. I ask for Your healing and transformation in this area of my life. Help me to see myself as You see me, beloved, chosen, and wonderfully made.

Holy Spirit, I invite You to work in my heart and mind. Teach me to embrace the identity You have given me in Christ, not based on my own abilities or failures, but on Your unchanging love and grace. Help me to listen to Your voice, which speaks truth and affirmation over me, and to reject the lies that try to define my worth.

Lord, I desire to grow deeper in my relationship with You, so that my sense of worth is rooted in Your love and not in the opinions of others or my own insecurities. Fill me with the confidence that comes from knowing I am Your child, and empower me to walk in the strength of Your Spirit. Help me to reflect Your love, joy, and peace, and to trust that You are continually shaping me into the person You have called me to be.

Thank You, Lord, for Your constant presence and for the Holy Spirit, who reminds me of my value in You. May I find my confidence and security in Your truth, knowing that I am enough because of what Christ has done for me.

In Jesus' name, I pray,

Amen!

Day Seven

ANGER AND FRUSTRATION

> *"Be angry and do not sin; do not let the sun go down on your anger."*
> **Ephesians 4:26**

Anger can easily take over and rule us if left unchecked or unnoticed, leading us away from God's peace. But the Holy Spirit gives us self-control and wisdom to be able to be better stewards over our emotions, preventing anger from taking root in our hearts and gaining authority over it.

The Relational Nature of the Holy Spirit

The Holy Spirit is not only a guide but also a comforting presence that helps us navigate our emotions, especially in times of anger and frustration. When you face these intense emotions, it's important to remember that the Holy Spirit is relational—meaning He meets us where we are, even in our struggles, and walks with us through them. One powerful scripture to hold onto is Galatians 5:22-23, which speaks of the fruits of the Spirit: "But the fruit of the Spirit is love, joy, peace, forbearance, kindness, goodness, faithfulness, gentleness and self-control." Anger and frustration can often feel isolating, but the Holy Spirit is an ever-present companion, providing both conviction and comfort. He enables us to pause, reflect, and remember the peace that God desires for us. Through the Spirit, we can transform these challenging emotions into moments of growth and grace, as He teaches us patience, humility, and self-control.

Cultivating Intimacy with the Holy Spirit

When deciding to develop intimacy with the Holy Spirit, especially when struggling with anger and frustration, it requires a heart willing to surrender and grow. Life's pressures can stir up emotions, but in those moments, we can find the Spirit's presence, guiding us to a place of peace and transformation. Begin by creating quiet moments, seeking God in prayer, and letting your heart be vulnerable before Him. The Holy Spirit is often described as a gentle counselor, one who comforts and heals. By inviting Him into our struggles, we allow Him to reveal the root of our anger and frustration. Acknowledge these feelings without judgment; remember, they are part of our humanity. But also believe that the Spirit can shape these emotions into something beautiful when surrendered to Him.

Understanding His Personality and Role

The Holy Spirit plays a powerful, personal role in uplifting and empowering us, especially when we struggle with self-esteem. Scripture reveals several traits and roles of the Holy Spirit that speak directly to those in need of encouragement and support such as our comforter, encourager, transformer, teacher, and truth-revealer. When struggling with self-esteem, leaning into the Holy Spirit's roles and presence can bring strength and peace. The Spirit continually reminds us that our worth is not based on what others think or even how we feel about ourselves but on the unwavering love God has for us. We are His beloved creation, with value beyond measure. Through the Holy Spirit, we can embrace that truth and grow in confidence, rooted in God's love.

Final Thoughts on Engaging with the Holy Spirit

Engaging with the Holy Spirit in moments of anger and frustration can be transformative. In those tense moments, pause and invite the Spirit to calm your heart. Remember, anger can cloud our vision, making it hard to see clearly, but the Holy Spirit is there to guide you back to peace, to remind you of who you truly are. This process of pausing, surrendering, and inviting the Spirit is a powerful act of humility, showing your openness to God's love and guidance.

REFLECTION QUESTIONS

What is the source of my anger, and how can I invite the Holy Spirit to heal those emotions?

_____

_____

_____

_____

_____

How can I respond to frustration with patience and understanding, trusting that the Holy Spirit will help me?

_____

_____

_____

_____

_____

How can I surrender my anger to God and trust His justice, knowing that I don't need to carry this burden alone?

_____

_____

_____

_____

_____

What does it look like to choose peace over conflict, and how can I invite the Holy Spirit to guide me in this?

_____

_____

_____

_____

_____

How can I practice self-control in my words and actions, even when I feel my emotions rising?

_____

_____

_____

_____

_____

PRACTICAL APPLICATION

Building a relationship with the Holy Spirit can be a powerful and transformative way to manage anger and frustration. Here is a practical application to help you along this journey, inspired by scripture:

Practice "Breathing in the Spirit"

When you feel anger or frustration rising, take a moment to breathe deeply. As you inhale, imagine you are breathing in the Holy Spirit, filling you with peace and clarity. As you exhale, release the tension and negative emotions. This simple act allows you to center yourself and invite the Spirit's peace. Each breath you take in that moment can be a reminder of God's proximity. The Holy Spirit is always near, offering help and comfort when you need it most.

PRAYER

Heavenly Father,

I come before You with a heart that seeks healing, guidance, and peace. Lord, I confess that anger and frustration often overwhelm me, and I know that these emotions hinder my growth and relationship with You. I pray for Your grace to help me overcome these struggles.

Holy Spirit, I invite You into my life in a deeper way. I ask You to fill me with Your presence and wisdom, to help me recognize the moments when anger begins to rise, and to give me the strength to pause and respond with love, patience, and understanding. Help me to surrender my frustrations to You and trust in Your timing and sovereignty.

Lord, I desire to be more like Christ—slow to anger and abounding in love. Teach me to reflect Your peace, and to rely on Your Spirit to transform my heart and mind. May Your presence become my constant source of comfort and strength.

I know that I cannot overcome these challenges on my own, but with You, all things are possible. Thank You for Your mercy and Your never-ending love. I trust You to work in me, to renew my spirit, and to guide me toward a life of peace and self-control.

In Jesus' name, I pray,

Amen!

REFERENCES

Holy Bible, King James Version

ABOUT THE AUTHOR

Nikayla Benbow

Nikayla A. Benbow is a testament to the transformative power of faith, resilience, and purpose. A graduate of Richland Northeast High School in Columbia, South Carolina, and Midlands Technical College, Nikayla is not only a single mother to a beautiful son Ra'Jon (13)—but also the founder of a life-changing nonprofit organization: The Safe Place MVMT.

As a survivor of life's many challenges, Nikayla knows firsthand the stigmas associated with the often-overlooked struggles that many of us have faced or may currently be facing. Her experiences have fueled her passion to create safe spaces where mothers, women, and men can heal, learn, and thrive. Through it all, she empowers others to embrace emotional healing, seek support, and rediscover their identity after hardship. Her message is simple yet profound: healing begins with honesty, vulnerability, and a supportive community.

Nikayla's ministry, The Safe Place MVMT, was born during one of the darkest moments of her life on February 21, 2022, when God gave her a vision of hope and restoration. This God-centered community brings women together from all walks of life, empowering them to find their voices, embrace their divine purpose, and break free from the chains of silence and shame. Nikayla's life verse is **Revelation 12:11**: *"They overcame him by the blood of the Lamb and by the word of their testimony."* She passionately reminds others that healing begins when we reveal our pain to God.

Her personal testimony is one of remarkable resilience. Nikayla has overcome the pain of domestic violence, childhood molestation, teenage pregnancy, toxic relationships, suicidal attempts, and identity struggles—all while serving faithfully in church and wearing a mask to hide her suffering. At her lowest point in 2021, she surrendered fully to God, began therapy, and rediscovered her worth. At 31 years old, she found her voice—and now, she uses it to inspire others.

Through her journey of healing, pruning, and redemption, Nikayla proclaims the beauty of "Life After." Life after postpartum depression. Life after trauma. Life after rejection. Her story is a powerful reminder that no matter how broken you feel, God's grace can restore and renew.

Nikayla's mission is to empower women and girls to uncover their truths, embrace God's healing, and become who they were created to be. Through faith, honesty, transparency, and community, she guides others to forgive themselves, grow, and walk boldly into their God-given destiny.

Her forever message is this: "There is more inside of you—you just haven't discovered it yet." Let's start the journey to the new together—with God leading the way.

www.ingramcontent.com/pod-product-compliance
Lightning Source LLC
LaVergne TN
LVHW061557070526
838199LV00077B/7081